JULIE BROWN

God's Promises are still true
# EVEN WHEN
A companion workbook

# Your Story

# Julie Brown

# FORWARD

When my wife died in the summer of 2019, I attended a Grief Share group and read many books on grief to better understand what I was experiencing and feeling with the death of my best friend. When my friend and colleague, Julie Brown, wrote a book on grief called, Even When, I wasn't sure I could read another book on grief. However, I am so glad I read the book. It was a quick read and impactful. I liked the organization: God is my provider, protector, and planner in every aspect of my life, physically, relationally, financially, and spiritually. Scripture came alive as Julie tied God Promises into every chapter. I found myself reflecting on my journey like Julie because of her illustrations and personal stories. I found myself laughing and crying many times as I read the book. After reading the book, I shared with Julie that I felt I needed to go deeper into my relationship with Jesus and the grief that I am continuing to experience.

I am so excited that Julie has written a companion workbook to her book, Even When. The workbook gives the reader the opportunity to delve into the scripture more deeply by understanding the context and content. The workbook also gives the reader the opportunity to assess where they are in the grief process and reflect on their personal journey. Finally, the workbook, through Julie's questions and reflections, will help the reader heal. Every person that has experienced a loss needs to get the book, Even When and the accompanying workbook. You will be glad you did.

Richard Rice

# HOW TO DIVE INTO THIS WORKBOOK

The sole purpose of this companion workbook is for you to remember how faithful God is and has been with you through your EVEN WHEN moment. It's designed so that you have something tangible to show the next generation about God's love and care for His people. I want you to tell your story of how faithful God has been through the fulfillment of His promises.

You (and this workbook) are a work in progress. Know that emotions are going to come. I cried tears of hopelessness when my EVEN WHEN moment happened, and I cried tears of gratefulness when I remembered how faithful God was to fulfill his promises. My emotions were like a rollercoaster, up one minute and down the next; however, my soul was not, simply because I knew that the rollercoaster had to come to base, at some time, on level ground. That's where I chose to land, on the solid foundation of God and His promises, and where His peace caused my soul to rest. Stop reading when you want. Take a breath and let the words sink in. Memorize the scripture. Write it down so the generations to come will know. And then, respond to the promises with a Yes and Amen.

*"May God give you more and more grace and peace as you grow in your knowledge of God and Jesus our Lord. By his divine power, God has given us everything we need for living a Godly life. We have received all of this by coming to know him, the*

*one who called us to himself by means of his marvelous glory and excellence. And because of his glory and excellence, he has given us great and precious promises. These are the promises that enable you to share his divine nature and escape the world's corruption caused by human desires. In view of all this, make every effort to respond to God's promises."* 2 Peter 1:2-5a (NLT)

*"For all of God's promises have been fulfilled in Christ with a resounding "Yes!" And through Christ, our "Amen" (which means "Yes") ascends to God for his glory."* 2 Corinthians 1:20 (NLT)

## NUTS AND BOLTS

There are five components to each promise:

1) The promise/scripture itself,

2) Researching the Scripture- through various Bible tools (commentaries, Greek translations, concordances), I've provided insight into the Scripture. I would encourage you to do the same and expound on any knowledge I've provided,

3) Revisiting the scripture- making the scripture your own by adding your EVEN WHEN moment into the promise,

4) Remembering- God gave you these promises in His precious Word. When you come to the Remembering section, allow God to remind you of how faithful He's been. If you can't think of anything to fill in the blank, leave it for now. Come back through the book and you'll be able to fill it

in then. If you read my book "EVEN WHEN" and did the homework at the end of each chapter, you may be able to transfer those thoughts to the Remembering section of each promise, and

5) Praying the scripture- this is my prayer for you. I would encourage you to write out your own prayer as well.

JULIE BROWN

## INTRO

Walking around my parents' property is like walking through generations of family history. My dad keeps a full-sized photo of my mom hanging on the wall of his woodworking area like a pinup girl from the 20's. It's actually her yearbook photo from when she was named Basketball Queen in 1960, tiara and all. He also has ice skates knotted around a nail that his dad used in the 1940's to pull around a sled. In the cabinets at the house, you can find my grandmother's china that she worked so hard to buy. My dad's military parade sword hangs by his desk. I've reminded my parents often to please write down the stories behind these items and tuck them into the folds, so we kids can remember and share with our kids, the lives entrenched in the fabric of these items. How else will our childrens' children know if we don't share the stories with them?

I have always journaled; from the time I was old enough to write until now. It came in spurts, though; I'd write for several days in my journal and then come back to it maybe a month, maybe a year, later. The things I wrote were personal feelings, ideas for stories, snippets of things I heard that I wanted to remember. I could turn back the pages and see how far I'd come in my life journey or how deep and scary the circumstances at that time were as recorded through my words on the page. My memory was refreshed when I looked at what I had written.

My book, *God's Promises are still true EVEN WHEN,* was written in the midst of grief. God carefully guided me through my darkest dark when my husband, Dennis, passed away. He whispered to me, sometimes with one word, other times with long breathy sentences. Often it was through friends and family. He was never silent as long as I kept my eyes on Him. I never wanted to forget the words He gave me, the promises He put in front of me to guide and comfort, the words He spoke to me. So, I wrote the book. Just like the items in my parents' house that had history wrapped around them, I wanted to keep His promises in the foreground of my thoughts.

There are reportedly thousands of promises between God and mankind in the Bible. Webster's Dictionary defines a promise as a noun that is a declaration or assurance that one will do a particular thing. As a verb, the definition is to assure someone that one will definitely do, give, or arrange something; undertake or declare that something will happen. Isn't it just like God to give us thousands upon thousands of promises in His Word? I am grateful that the omnipresent and all-knowing God: 1) He gave these promises to us, and 2) He had scribes write them down, so that generations later, we can still be reminded of who God is and what He says He will do.

When I finished writing EVEN WHEN, God continued to speak to me. In His goodness and perfectness, He said "Now share it. Tell others. Remind them that I care for them, too. My promises are still true regardless of the circumstances. Regardless of their failures, accomplishments, or challenges. Show them how to write their story of My faithfulness."

Just like the scribes of old wrote down the stories of God's love for us to read and remember from generation to generation, here we are, together, writing your story. EVEN WHEN the darkest of dark happens, you will have this workbook to remind you that He who has always been there, will always be with you.

*"You are faithful to fulfill every promise you've made."* Psalm 145:13b (TPT)

JULIE BROWN

## My Story → Your Story

If you're reading this, chances are you've experienced grief and loss or are possibly walking through it right now. There's no timeline for grief. You're not going to be "better" after time goes by. You're going to be different, different perspective, different reality.

The first thing I want you to know is God created each of us uniquely. You may try to brush off your EVEN WHEN moment as "it's not as bad as yours (losing Dennis)." To this I say again, you are uniquely created by God. Your EVEN WHEN moments will not be my EVEN WHEN moments, or anyone else's. Because you're you, not me. We may have the same experience of losing a spouse, but you will not respond the same way I did because I'm just as unique as you are. There may be the prescribed stages of grief (denial, anger, bargaining, depression, acceptance) that we go through, but you will not go through them at my pace or respond the way I respond. Grief looks different on E.V.E.R.Y.O.N.E. My loss is not greater or less than yours- just unique.

**My Story**- My EVEN WHEN moment happened on Saturday, March 13, 2021. Dennis passed away after a three-year battle with cancer just shy of our 24th wedding anniversary. Grief wasn't on my radar, and loss was the last thing I wanted to write about in my journal.

**Your Story**- Let's start by naming your EVEN WHEN moment, the specific time when grief and loss collided in your life. It could be a series of events, but most likely, it's the last one in the series. The heart-wrenching, hard to breathe, "not sure I can live through this" moment. It could be a loved one has passed on, or you didn't get the job/promotion you really thought you deserved. The death of a dream, a relationship lost, hope extinguished with the perception of "nothing's going to change" or "it wasn't supposed to be this way".

*"But when anything is exposed by the light, it becomes visible,"* Ephesians 5:13 (ESV)

Name it. Call it out into the light. Write it down.

Having trouble identifying your EVEN WHEN moment? Let's talk, right here in my living room. Why are you sad? Why are you angry? What disrupted your life so much that things that are supposed to be easy, just aren't? Drop some words in the space above; words that may pull your EVEN WHEN moment out of the darkness.

You've named it, now what? Counseling? Coffee with a friend? Loud sobbing at the altar? If you need to. If you need counseling or medication or peaceful rest (a nap doesn't cut soul-weariness), do it. This guided workbook is only another tool in your toolbox. It's not designed as counseling or as a step in your grief stage.

My encouragement to you is to stop right here and take it to Jesus. He already knows. Pray for His protection, His guidance, and His mercy and grace as you walk this out. Pray for "revelation-knowledge" as the Passion translation (TPT) calls it.

As you go through this book, you are likely to do the "one step forward, two steps backward" dance. It's okay as long as Jesus is your partner. He's not a wallflower waiting on the fringes, not involved. He's got His name plastered all over your dance card.

Ask any person right after a loss (or their EVEN WHEN moment) for one word that sums up how they are feeling. You'll hear a variety of words: lost, scared, anxious, confused, sad, devastated to name a few. My word was "unsafe", not physically unsafe, but emotionally unsafe. My confidant, debate partner, decision-maker husband was gone. I had to make choices and decisions on my own with no one to bounce ideas with. As I called that which was in darkness (being unsafe) out into the light, God met me right there.

In my story, God laid out His promises in three distinct categories, all surrounding my unsafe feeling: 1) He was my provider, 2) my protector, and 3) my planner. He gave me scripture after scripture and dropped them into those categories.

This is your story, so we'll start with your word. List in the space provided, a word or phrase that describes you right now or when your EVEN WHEN moment happened.

We'll come back to that word or phrase as we dive into the promises.

## GOD IS GOOD AND FAITHFUL
He promises you.

*"For the Lord is good. His unfailing love continues forever, and his faithfulness continues to each generation."* Psalm 100:5 (NLT)

### Researching the Scripture

*"For the Lord is good."*- Good in Hebrew means valuable in estimation or excellent.

*"His unfailing love continues forever"*- "continuous existence" is how His love is described. It's not going anywhere. It was here before, it's here now, and it will be here forever.

*"And His faithfulness continues to each generation."*- I get that faithfulness can be intertwined with trust, but I've never thought of the other words that the Hebrew brings in: steadiness and firmness.

I started the promises with this scripture because I need (and you do, too) to know Who is giving me all of these promises. Talk is cheap, as I like to say, and you really can't trust every promise from every person. People hand promises out like candy and then there's no follow through or just empty words. The rest of the phrase "talk is cheap and actions speak louder" resonates better with me. If you give me a promise and you act on that promise by following through, I will trust your promises. God has proven over and over with multiple actions- some at that same time- that He is faithful, good, trustworthy, and kind. For always, and for every generation. Choose to revisit this scripture often as it is one of the blocks of your foundation on which all of His promises sit.

## Revisiting the Scripture

Example: EVEN WHEN my husband dies, God gives me promises that I can trust, promises that will never end, promises that are handed down through the generations.

Your story (write out the scripture following your EVEN WHEN moment as in the example): EVEN WHEN

### Remembering

God fulfills His promises whether you trust Him or not. That's Truth with a capital "T". He's already given the promises, and He's already acted on them; we just need to receive Him. Thinking back, was there ever a time when you said, "Okay God, you've given me all of these promises (or this one in particular), and I trust you to fulfill them." Write that moment down in the space allotted. Add how you felt when you made that decision.

**Praying the Scripture**

Father, thank you for being good and kind and trustworthy. All of my days (and EVEN WHEN those moments occur), I will trust you. You have proven your love to the generations before me and the ones after me. I will trust in the promises you have for me.

Yes, and Amen.

JULIE BROWN

## GOD WILL NEVER LEAVE YOU
He promises you.

*"It is the Lord who goes before you. He will be with you; He will not leave you or forsake you. Do not fear or be dismayed."* Deuteronomy 31:8 (ESV)

### Researching the Scripture

*"It is the Lord who goes before you."*- No one else has the foresight to go ahead of us. In this Scripture, it's really talking about His presence going (action) ahead of our EVEN WHEN moment and being there before we are.

*"He will be with you"*- Just like He always has been.

*"He will not leave you or forsake you"*- Therein lies the promise, just as He has done in the past, He will not leave you behind, but will go ahead of you. His presence will never forsake you.

*"Do not"*- this is our action. The verbs that come after will be important!

*"Be afraid or discouraged"*- The Hebrew translates this first verb as fear or to dread something. "Discouraged," also translated from the Hebrew means dismayed or shattered, broken.

The NLT translation says this scripture this way:

"Do not be afraid or discouraged, for the Lord will personally go before you." You might have missed it. A little word amongst the giants in this scripture. For. Just a three-letter word. Somewhat insignificant until you research what the word "for" in the Bible means. The word "for" in simple terms means "in place of" or "a substitute".

For your fear and discouragement, He wants to substitute good news! He's already gone before you! And coupled with His promise to never fail you, nor abandon you, why give in to those feelings of fear and discouragement?

I'm certain there has been a time in your life where you felt afraid and discouraged. It's hard not to in this day and age. Can you look back on a time and say, "I didn't see it at the time, but now I can. God went before me in that situation?" Write it down in the allotted space so you can remember.

### Revisiting the Scripture

Example: EVEN WHEN I feel like everyone else has left me and I'm feeling alone, God promises to personally go ahead of me. He promises to be with me; He promises He will neither fail me nor abandon me.

Your story (write out the scripture following your EVEN WHEN moment as in the example): EVEN WHEN

### Remembering
Can you think of a time after your EVEN WHEN moment, that God fulfilled this promise to you? For me, it was all the times after Dennis died that someone would approach me and say "God sees you". He knew those specific words from a variety of people would show me He was still watching and present in my life. How has God shown you that He will never leave you?

### Praying the Scripture
Father, Thank you for never failing or abandoning me. I may be afraid and discouraged in circumstances and through my EVEN WHEN moments, but you've already substituted your way into my way. You've already gone ahead of me.

Yes, and Amen.

## NOTHING CAN SEPARATE YOU FROM GOD'S LOVE
He promises you.

*"And I am convinced that nothing can ever separate us from God's love. Neither death nor life, neither angels nor demons, neither our fears for today nor our worries about tomorrow—not even the powers of hell can separate us from God's love. No power in the sky above or in the earth below— indeed, nothing in all creation will ever be able to separate us from the love of God that is revealed in Christ Jesus our Lord."* Romans 8:38-39 (NLT)

### Researching the Scripture
*"And I am convinced"*- the "I" in this verse is Paul writing one of his letters (Romans) to comfort the church and yet, also bring a challenge. He's already talked earlier in this chapter about if God's love was so great that He gave up His son for us, who else (or what) is greater than that love? He's also talked about how God made them conquerors over all. More than Conquerors; the Greek word that describes us is *hupernikao* or a glorious hyper-victory!

*"That nothing can ever separate us from God's*

*love*"- To divide or put away from. Look at the list below- that's everything under the sun (and above it) that cannot move us away from God's love.

"*Neither death nor life*"- Death refers to the separation of the body from the soul. Life refers to the living, breathing soul and body. I read it as when life gets busy, and I forget my purpose here on earth is to honor and glorify Him in everything I do (aka I forget to commune or abide with Him), He doesn't say "Well, today I'm going to separate my love from her." Thank God… literally.

"*Neither angels nor demons*"- I always thought it would be cool to have an angel swoop down and confirm a life step or a big decision for me until I read how often they start with "Do not be afraid" and then I would rethink that thought. Angels in this scripture's Greek translation means a messenger, could be a messenger from God or could be a pastor that's providing a message to the church. Regardless of the messenger, either from God or hell-nor the message itself, can separate you from God's love.

"*Neither our fears for today nor our worries about tomorrow*"- Pretty clear cut. Nothing that is happening today or tomorrow.

"*Not even the powers of hell can separate us from God's love*"- Not even the mighty powers that are from hell itself.

"*No power in the sky above or in the earth below*"- "Deep and wide, deep and wide", remember that Sunday school song? Some translations say "no height nor depth can separate us".

"*Indeed, nothing in all creation will ever be able to separate us from the love of God*"- Nothing. No created thing will be able to separate us.

*"That is revealed in Christ Jesus our Lord."*-Coming from God as established in the sacrifice of His son.

The Matthew Henry commentary sums this Scripture up beautifully: "Be they ever so great and strong, ever so many, ever so mighty, ever so malicious, what can they do? While God is for us, and we keep in his love, we may with a holy boldness defy all the powers of darkness. Let Satan do his worst, he is chained; let the world do its worst, it is conquered: principalities and powers are spoiled and disarmed, and triumphed over, in the cross of Christ."[1]

After all I've read in the Bible, and all I've seen with my own two eyes, and with everything I know about the love of God, I am convinced/sure/persuaded of this, too!

### Revisiting the Scripture

EXAMPLE: EVEN WHEN my spouse leaves and his present love is removed from my life, God's love is eternal and there isn't one created thing that can change that.

Your Story (write out the scripture following your EVEN WHEN moment as in the example):

---

[1]https://www.blueletterbible.org/Comm/mhc/Rom/Rom_00 8.cfm?a=1054038

### Remembering

Can you think of a time after your EVEN WHEN moment that you simply felt unlovable? Maybe you were angry and said some things you shouldn't have. Maybe, like with my EVEN WHEN moment, the person who said "I love you" the most (aside from maybe your parents) went to be with Jesus. Maybe your actions have caused you to walk away from God. Regardless, God still loves you and NOTHING can separate you from that love. Write down that time when you discovered, or it was revealed to you, how nothing can separate you from God's love.

### Praying the Scripture

Father, I know it's me when I feel far from you. I know, from this scripture, that nothing said or done or coming from any created thing can separate me from Your love. When I begin to feel distant or cut off from You, remind me to spend time with you, to make you a priority. Thank you for never retracting Your love for me.

Yes and Amen

## GOD WILL ALWAYS PROVIDE
He promises you.

*"Yahweh is my best friend and my shepherd. I always have more than enough."* Psalm 23:1 (TPT)

*"For the Lord God is brighter than the brilliance of a sunrise! Wrapping himself around me like a shield, he is so generous with his gifts of grace and glory. Those who walk along his paths with integrity will never lack one thing they need, for he provides it all!"* Psalm 84:11 (TPT)

### Researching the Scripture

*"Yahweh is my best friend"*- Have you ever thought of God as your best friend? The one you call first when things go right, or things go wrong, or just to talk about things? My closest friends are people I can trust, who are loyal and speak truth to me; who check in on me and who I look forward to seeing each time we meet. If Jesus is our best friend and we respect Him as such, He should be the first person we turn to, not our friends or family.

"*My shepherd*"- I am in definite need of a shepherd. I often second guess myself, ponder for hours about my decisions, and turn a situation over and over in my mind, trying to see all sides. Many of my friends are quick problem solvers and can make speedy decisions. That is not me. Knowing that I have a shepherd who is aware of my past and future and who has a plan for my life, I can rest easy in my journey as long as I listen for His voice and follow His guidance.

"*Wrapping Himself around me like a shield*"- I love this visual image. Shields in Biblical times were usually large wooden panels, strengthened with metal plates or studs, and covered the person from head to toe. If God is wrapping Himself around me, that means my sides are covered, too. Shields in any era were used for protection. A person could protect himself from close-range combat or gather with others and it offered more widespread protection from fiery darts flying overhead.

"*Walk along His paths with integrity*"- I like to walk on paths with solid footing, ones with a clear view of what's up ahead, but it doesn't always happen that way. Pinecones and acorns, slithering creatures I'd rather not speak of, and scrub trees with thorns do not make for easy hiking. But hearing the breeze whisper through the trees or a hint of pine or wildflowers in the air makes for an easy hike. How do you know you're on His path, though? Follow His commandments, read His word, spend time with Him, and He will direct your path. Doors will open, red flags will pop up, and most often, the yellow ribbons marking the path will guide you.

*"Will never lack one thing"*- Pretty self-explanatory, except we often feel like we are lacking in some area. Maybe you feel like you're lacking in money or friends or ministry gifts. Is it possible that God doesn't believe you are lacking and the aforementioned wants are not for you at this time? If He says you will NEVER lack one thing, but you believe you need a boyfriend/girlfriend, is that your need? Of course it is. God says He will always provide for you, so maybe your need doesn't line up with God's promises, OR it's not the right time.

### Revisiting the Scripture
Example: EVEN WHEN my life is in shambles, I know I can come to you as my best friend and shepherd, and you will provide more than enough.

Your Story: (write out the scripture following your EVEN WHEN moment as in the example)

### Remembering
There have been many times when I thought "This is such a mess. How'd it ever get to this point?" It was during those times that I realized I'd been trying to do it by my own strength, not consulting God, and not even aware that He may have something better for me. I just forged on. Can you think of a time where if you had just stopped to listen, or ask, where God wanted to lead you that you would be in a much different spot and mind frame? Write that time down and remember how He provided for you.

**Praying the Scripture**

Father, thank you for being my best friend and for leading me on Your path. Wrap yourself around me like a shield and be generous with your gifts of grace. Allow me to overflow with abundance in every good thing I do for your glory. Thank you for your overwhelming care and love for my needs.

Yes and Amen.

## GOD PROVIDES REST
He promises you.

*"Come to me, all who labor and are heavy laden, and I will give you rest."* Matthew 11:28 (ESV)

Same Scripture in the Passion Translation-
*"Are you weary, carrying a heavy burden? Come to me. I will refresh your life, for I am your oasis."*

### Researching the Scripture

*"Come to me"*- An action on our part; we have to be willing to say, "I can't do this on my own" and GO to Him. He already knows, He just wants you to come to Him.

*"All who labor and are heavy laden"*- Too tired to do anything? Weary from all that life has thrown at you? Exhausted? We're not talking about what a short power nap could do for you. We're talking about clench-your-teeth, holding-on-for-too-long, don't-care weary.

*"And I will give you rest"*- He will stop the burdens and hardness of life's toils and will refresh you, so you can pick up and go again about His business.

This Scripture, in context with the surrounding Scriptures, is really wanting you to shake off the heaviness that sin brings into your life, to stop battling against flesh and blood enemies and take up His armor, to put on His yoke (v. 29-30) that is light and easy. Not an easy button, but like the Passion translation puts it, "I am your oasis." When we come to Him with our weary soul and give it all to Him, He promises to give us the rest we so desire.

### Revisiting the Scripture
Example- EVEN WHEN the world has become too overwhelming, I know I can go to Jesus and He will provide the rest I need from all of the questions, expectations, and weariness of my soul.

Your Story (write out the scripture following your EVEN WHEN moment as in the example):

### Remembering
Can you think of a time after your EVEN WHEN moment that God provided you with an oasis, a moment of rest? I had to visualize taking off the yoke of sadness and laying it at Jesus' feet and then exchanging it with His yoke. Write it down in the space allotted so you will always remember and can share it with others.

### Praying the Scripture
Father, thank you that you are so aware of the trials we face in this world. Some we've created in this busy life of ours and some from the fiery darts of

the enemy. You already knew we'd need peace and an oasis to rest in. Thank you for meeting us in our weariness.

Yes and Amen

## GOD IS WORKING EVERYTHING OUT FOR GOOD
He promises you.

*"And we know that God causes everything to work together for the good of those who love God and are called according to His purpose for them."* Romans 8:28 (NLT)

### Researching the Scripture

*"And"*- the standard word in the English language to indicate that something of importance to the latter came before the "and" and is connected to it. So, what does the Scripture before say? We could start there, but it also has an "and" at the start of it as does the next one (with a "but" in between) and likewise for the scripture above that one. You'll need to start with v. 24 to get v. 28 in context. I'll let you read those.

*"We know"*- If I "know" something, I'm usually pretty confident about it. I've studied it, observed it, and pondered it. I've used all of my senses to perceive it. Basically, the author is saying "you've already decided this thing, and I'm just reminding you."

*"That God causes everything to work together"*- Note to self: the words EVERYTHING and

TOGETHER.

"*For the good of those who love God*"-
Remember, this is God causing this, and He doesn't
lie. Good is relative in our world- I want to have a
good job, I want my kids to be good, I want a good
life. God's "good" is agreeable, honorable, excellent,
and a benefit. Not a feeling or a want.

"*And are called according to His purpose for
them*"- I have heard this word ("called") used
incorrectly so many times that I always have to go
back to the Greek to confirm what it means. In this
Scripture, "called" means to be invited (like to a
banquet) or divinely selected or appointed. He has
invited you to be Holy and in commune with Him.
"His purpose"- People struggle with their purpose in
life, however, this Scripture says "*His* purpose for
*them*." Coupled with "good" and "called," I think we
can safely say that God is inviting us to be with Him
and He is setting forth (the Greek word "*prothesis*")
the plans and purposes He has for us. Perfectly lines
up with everything else we "know" about God.

### Revisiting the Scripture

EXAMPLE: EVEN WHEN my husband dies, I
know that God wants good in my life (not temporary
things, but eternal things) and has invited me to be a
part of the purposes He has already established or set
forth.

Your Story (write out the scripture following
your EVEN WHEN moment as in the example):

## Remembering

Long ago, I had so many plans for my future- to go to college, to get married, to have a child or two- all things good for my life. When my EVEN WHEN moment happened and Dennis died, dark thoughts entered my arena. What now? All of those good things had happened, but now this bad thing came in and caused me to question what good could come of this- of me- now. But God in His infinite wisdom allowed me to see that His good for my life were more eternal things, and those actions were still in play. Do you remember a time after your EVEN WHEN moment thinking, "This can't be a good plan?" And then He shows you that yes, this is still a good plan. From His perspective. Write that time down in the space allotted so you can be reminded of His faithfulness.

## Praying the Scripture

Father, thank you for always working good for us even if we don't see it. Help us to clearly see how you've invited us to be a part of a purpose bigger than ourselves. I give you control to do and see and know what is best for me.

Yes and Amen

JULIE BROWN

## LEAN ON GOD FOR UNDERSTANDING
He promises you.

*"Trust in the Lord with all your heart, and do not lean on your own understanding."* Proverbs 3:5 (ESV)

### Researching the Scripture
*"Trust in the Lord"*- Whoa, trust is a tricky thing. But trust in the Lord results in confidence and a secure feeling, unlike faith in mankind whose emotions rule their decisions and motives ruin their reputations.

*"With all your heart"*- Totally. Not the 80's word, but with totality, every inch. Heart in the Hebrew is *"lēḇ"* and refers not to the organ that pumps blood inside your body, but the inner man (your soul, mind, and will). Make everything in you trust in the Lord.

*"And do not lean"*- Don't trust…

*"On your own understanding."*- Your own discernment, thought, knowledge.

### Revisiting the Scripture
EXAMPLE: EVEN WHEN my reality doesn't match my expectations, You promise us that if we trust you and not our own understanding that you will

take care of us.

Your Story (write out the scripture following your EVEN WHEN moment as in the example):

### Remembering

I did not understand how my husband dying was a good plan for me. My heart (emotions) was broken. I did not understand. I simply had to trust Him and not look at the circumstances and He promised to take care of me. Do you remember a time (probably after your EVEN WHEN moment) that you truly didn't understand, but knew deep down inside, that you had to trust your Heavenly Father to take care of you? Write that time down in the allotted space.

### Praying the Scripture

Father, we often don't understand why things happen the way they do. It's beyond our comprehension. Thank you for being an all-knowing God, an all-seeing God, and an always-present God. We trust your character, your faithfulness, and your love for us. Help me to not lean into my own understanding. Help me to lean into you.

Yes and Amen

## GOD HAS A PLAN FOR YOU
He promises you.

*"The heart of man plans his way, but the Lord establishes his steps."* Proverbs 16:9 (ESV)

*"For I know the plans I have for you,"*
*declares the Lord, "plans to prosper you and not to*
*harm you, plans to give you hope and a future."*
Jeremiah 29:11 (NIV)

### Researching the Scripture
*"The heart of man plans his way"*- I have lots of plans; I'm sure you do, too. Plans on what to eat for the week, calendar dates on my phone, lists of my goals and how to reach those goals. Your plans may not be as extensive or detailed as mine are, but you've got plans. Sometimes they actually happen and sometimes they stay in my head until they either get bumped out for new plans, or the moment has passed, and they need to be laid to rest (like my new year's resolutions that don't seem to make it past the first week of January). "Heart" in this scripture means "inner man" which includes our mind or intellect, our feelings, our soul, and our will. It's much bigger than just your heart and much, much bigger than the plans you may have laid out for

yourself. Our motives and inclinations also figure into our "heart", and I think we can all agree that our plans are often selfish and maybe (dare I say it?) not born of God's plans for our lives.

"*But*"- Love this word, especially in the Bible. The King James Version dictionary defines "but" as a separation or exception.[2] How cool that even if we set our own plans in motion, and if we continually ask for His involvement, His plans will prevail.

"*The Lord establishes his steps*"- Have you ever walked along the beach and you're acutely aware of where the hard-packed sand ends and the shifting sand begins? I can walk with shoes or flip flops on the sand right above where the water breaks with no problem, but I'm always a little leery of the sand that ebbs and flows underfoot. In this promise, the Lord says He will establish your steps. "To establish" means to make firm, to make secure, and to settle; one word with three very comforting meanings. My plans and decisions may crumble like a cookie that I left in the oven too long, BUT His plans for my life journey are already secured.

"*For I know*"- He already knows! He knows the plans He has in store for you. He knows that you may have plans for you. He knows the decisions that you will make and the thoughts you will have and the steps you will take to get there. He already knows.

"*The plans I have for you*"- Normally, I don't look to the King James Version (KJV) for anything, but I stumbled onto this very different translation. The KJV says "the thoughts I think about you". Back

---

[2] https://av1611.com/kjbp/kjv-dictionary/but.html

up and read that again. This is in the Bible, written by men many, many years ago and God just confirmed in His Word that He has thoughts about you…twice in one Scripture.

*"Declares the Lord"*- A declaration or revelation from the Lord Himself.

*"Plans to prosper you and not to harm you"*- I love the word prosper; it sounds like a word that I want to print in big letters and hang on my refrigerator. Usually, people think the word "prosper" has to do with financial success, and it does, with many other connotations as well. I want to "become strong and flourishing"[3] in my health, in the peace I dwell in, and in my overall welfare. I'm sure you do, too. Thriving in my emotional or physical well-being is so much more important to me than my financial stability.

*"Plans to give you hope and a future."*- In digging a little deeper in this scripture, I discovered another Scripture that complements this one- Hebrews 6:19a "We have this certain hope like a strong, unbreakable anchor holding our souls to God himself." (TPT) The hope that He gives not only anchors our souls, but creates a "cord" connecting us to Him. I am expectantly looking forward with hope to the plans and thoughts He has for me.

### Revisiting the Scripture

Example: EVEN WHEN my already mapped out plans failed, YOU had already established Your

---

[3] https://www.merriam-webster.com/dictionary/prosper

plans for my future; plans for physical, emotional, relational prosperity, thoughts of well-being and not of harm.

Your story (write out the scripture following your EVEN WHEN moment as in the example):

### Remembering

After your EVEN WHEN moment, it can be really difficult to believe that there is a plan or that God is thinking about you. It's much easier to get caught up in the sorrow and to not think about anything for a bit. Sometimes people have to tell you to take a shower or to eat. God, in His infinite wisdom, gives you this promise: He already knows the plans He has for you. He knew this EVEN WHEN moment would happen. And though you might not see Him at work right now, He cannot go back on His promise. Has God given you a glimpse of His thoughts toward you? His plans that He has already established? Write them in the area allotted so you can remember them.

### Praying the Scripture

Father, Your ways are so much different than our ways. Your thoughts are so much deeper than ours. Thank you for planning out my days and giving me purpose here on this earth. Establish my steps so that I can do Your will. Thank you for this promise and all it holds for me.

Yes and Amen

# EVEN WHEN

## GOD GIVES STRENGTH
He promises you.

*"He gives power to the faint, and to him who has no might he increases strength."* Isaiah 40:29 (ESV)

### Researching the Scripture

*"He gives power to the faint"*- Some translations use the word "strength" in place of "power" which is the Hebrew word *"kōaḥ"*. Either way, God is bestowing on you strength and His power, not of human power, to the faint, exhausted, weary people. I get faint keeping up with teenagers (my ministry within the church), but this is more than that; in my opinion, it's the exhaustion that comes from trying to be what others want or the expectations you have placed on yourself. It's the world pressing in on every side and having to be "on guard" against all of those fiery darts thrown at you by the enemy.

*"And to him who has no might He increases strength"*- Increases-enlarges-multiplies. This "strength" is a different Hebrew word than the one earlier in the scripture; this one is *"āṣmâ"* which also means power and might but adds a twist. This *"āṣmâ"* includes an abundance of strength and power and rounds it out with an extension, per se.

God not only provides strength to us weary people, but He provides it in abundance and as an extension of His own glorious power and strength.

**Revisiting the Scripture**
EXAMPLE: EVEN WHEN my world is spinning and spiraling, You've promised to give me strength, Your strength. So very needed.

Your Story (write out the scripture following your EVEN WHEN moment as in the example):

**Remembering**
On those nights (it was usually night), I could sit and look out the window and just think…about nothing. Many minutes would go by before I realized I was just staring out into the yard, but I didn't have the energy to do one. more. thing. I'd haul myself off to bed (or change positions on the couch because the bed was empty) and hope tomorrow would bring the energy to do a little more. Every single time, I'd wake up and be able to do one thing, even if that one thing was making a goal to do one thing. He increased my strength slowly and at my pace because He loved me. Can you remember a time when you were so weary that "one more thing" was just too much, but you asked God for the strength to help you? And He did? Write that in the space allotted so you will remember His promise to you.

**Praying the Scripture**

Father, we are so thankful that when our EVEN WHEN moment happens, you have promised us that we don't have to have the strength to do one more thing. You have the strength we need and it's simply an extension of your own power. Thank you for lifting our countenance, our souls, our bodies to have the strength to go on and to move forward in the plans you have for us.

Yes and Amen

JULIE BROWN

## GOD'S GRACE AND SUFFICIENCY ARE YOURS.
He promises you.

*"Yes, God is more than ready to overwhelm you with every form of grace, so that you will have more than enough of everything- every moment and in every way. He will make you overflow with abundance in every good thing you do."* 2 Corinthians 9:8 (TPT)

### Researching the Scripture
*"Yes, God is more than ready"*- He is able, He has the power to do so, and He is READY.

*"To overwhelm you"*- Overwhelmed- swamped- engulfed- inundated. The word itself sounds overwhelming! When was the last time you were overwhelmed by something or someone? The Greek word for overwhelm is *perisseuõ* which means to overflow, or to over and above, and to be in abundance. Don't you want to be overwhelmed by God today?

*"With every form of grace"*- All, each and every form. I usually get grace and mercy slightly confused. Grace, according to John Piper, is an undeserved favor, but it can also embrace the truth that "this favor overflows in powerful, practical

helpfulness from God in your daily life where you most need it. That help is also called grace because it's free and it's undeserved.[4]

"*So that you'll have more than enough of everything, every moment and in every way*"- Everything? Really? That's what this promise says? Yes.

"*He will make you overflow with abundance in every good thing you do.*" I love to take scripture and dissect it, draw circles around the verbs, underline the big words, but I also know how important it is to not take a Scripture out of context. Read the Scriptures before and behind it so you know the entire picture of what God is promising. In this Scripture, He is talking to the cheerful giver, the one who gives generously and without being reluctant or pressured. So the promise is to those who give abundantly (either time, money, or treasure), He will cause you to overflow in these areas. If you give freely, He will overwhelm you with all forms of grace with everything.

### Revisiting the Scripture

Example: EVEN WHEN my decisions are off course, but I give freely of my treasures like we're taught to, God has promised to overwhelm me with grace, in every form, in every moment, and in every way.

Your Story (write out the scripture following

---

your EVEN WHEN moment as in the example):

### Remembering
At birthdays and Christmas time, I am the worst at buying presents. I can't just pick something up and think, "This is a good gift for someone, don't know who, but someone will like it." That is just not me. I have to agonize over what that person would like, what would bring that person the most joy. I get almost frantic- I'm not a good shopper, either- until I find the. perfect. gift. How like our Heavenly Father to give us good gifts (knowing the perfect gift) and give it to overflowing. Just what we need, just when we need it. Can you think of a time when God not only gave you a gift, but gave it overwhelmingly? Over the top, unexpectedly? Write it down so you'll remember how good God is.

### Praying the Scripture
Father, thank you for being more than ready to overwhelm us with your goodness. You multiply everything over and above what we can imagine so that we can overflow Your goodness into other's lives. I love the idea of overflowing with abundance. Remind me to tell others of Your faithfulness so they can be as overwhelmed as I am.
     Yes and Amen

## GOD WILL ALWAYS PROTECT
He promises you.

*"Even when your path takes me through the valley of deepest darkness, fear will never conquer me, for you already have! Your authority is my strength and my peace. The comfort of your love takes away my fear."* Psalm 23:4-5 (TPT)

### Researching the Scripture

*"Even when"*- Here are the words that started it all. "Even" is used as an intensifier of the word it precedes according to many commentaries. In other versions, this Scripture starts with "Yea" which means "truly" or is used as an affirmative word.

*"Your path takes me"*- This requires us to stay on the path and go. Not lament over where the path is going. Again, His path is the one we must choose.

*"Through"*- Not stopping at the beginning or halfway, but going all the way to the end. I'm often reminded of my favorite movie, "The Wizard of Oz", and how Dorothy had to follow the yellow brick road to reach her goal (seeing the wizard). Her path took her through some pretty dark woods, and she encountered horrible, evil people (the witch), but the author complemented her journey with very loyal and supportive companions. She had to go through

the woods, despite having apples thrown at her, and had to go through the poppy field, fighting the deep intoxicating sleep pressing in on her. This Scripture, while it goes so much deeper than Dorothy's story, emphasizes that there is an end to the path, the road that holds so much danger, despair, and darkness.

*"The valley of deepest darkness"*- The valley suggests that we are hemmed in on all sides, not on an open path where we can breathe easily and deeply, but closed in from every direction. David, in the original text, could have been thinking about steep slopes surrounding him that blocked out the sun most of the day or from a militaristic way where the enemies on the hill tops threaten death from above, We've all been to that place, though, that deepest darkness where our emotional state borders on hopelessness and circumstances look very bleak. Rock bottom, nowhere but up, and up sometimes feels impossible.

*"Fear will never conquer me, for you already have"*- What good news! Despite all the darkness, the struggle to stay upright, and the challenges barricading our path, He has already gone before you. He didn't clear the path, He just said your fear will not conquer you. He also didn't say you won't have fear, but rather that it won't swallow you up and make you ineffective, frozen in place, rendered useless.

*"Your authority is my strength and peace. The comfort of your love takes away my fear."*- His authority over all of the heavens and earth, that's what gets you through the dark places and gives you strength to go through life. Knowing His authority

reigns supreme should bring you the "peace of God that surpasses all understanding." (Philippians 4:7 ESV) His unfailing love blankets and extinguishes all fear so that you can operate in His power and for His glory.

### Revisiting the Scripture

Example: EVEN WHEN I lose a loved one to death, and your path takes me through the valley of deepest darkness, fear will not conquer me, for you already have conquered death! EVEN WHEN my husband dies, your authority will be my strength and peace, and the comfort of your love will take away my fear.

YOUR Story: (write out the scripture following your EVEN WHEN moment as in the example)

### Remembering

Dark were those nights, listening to my husband desperately try to breathe in the bed we'd made for him in the living room. Or when we sat through another round of bad news. Or when I was making funeral arrangements. They were dark, dark times for me. I worshiped in the back room with my keyboard and God. I prayed and fasted. I played music too loud when I couldn't quiet the fear scrambling from my heart into my throat. I didn't want to make plans for AFTER. After Dennis died. If I didn't make those plans, maybe it wouldn't happen. I fought fear for the last three months of his life. And always, ALWAYS,

God provided something or someone to walk beside me, pulling me along through the deepest darkness. God promised to protect me, give me strength, and to comfort me. And He did just that. Can you think of a time during your EVEN WHEN moment when God met you right where you were on that dark path, guiding, comforting, protecting you? Write it down in the space allotted.

### Praying the Scripture

Father, thank you. Thank you for caring and loving me enough to protect and comfort me through my EVEN WHEN moment. You already knew it would happen, you set me upon that path, and you knew that you would walk me through it, too. You promise that the deepest darkness cannot consume me; remind me of that when fear comes knocking, and I forget that you've already overcome it. Thank you for your peace and strength.

Yes and Amen

## GOD MEETS YOUR NEEDS
He promises you.

*"And this same God who takes care of me will supply all your needs from His glorious riches, which have been given to us in Christ Jesus."*
Philippians 4:19 (NLT)

### Researching the Scripture
*"And this same God who takes care of me"*- He's the same God for you and for me if you're a believer. There's no other God.

*"Will supply"*- Supply in the Greek is the word "plēroō" which means to furnish liberally and so that nothing shall be left wanting, but to full measure. Not just a "here's your portion," but your cup is full to the brim. There's no room for any more.

*"All your needs"*- Needs, not wants. We so often confuse the two because we think we must have this or that to sustain life. You know the difference, it's just hard not to want the wants!

*"From His glorious riches"*- His abundance of wealth that exceeds our expectations.

*"Which have been given to us in Christ Jesus"*- He's already ready for your needs. He's just waiting for you to ask.

This Scripture is often taken out of the context in which it was written, but we can infer that it is for us, too, in this day and age. Chapter 4 of Philippians is a part of a letter to the people of Philippi from Paul who was imprisoned in their city for preaching the gospel. After the miracle of the prison doors flying open and the jailor being saved, a church was planted in Philippi. The people were gracious and kind to Paul as he stayed in their city and throughout his travels. They were near to his heart, and he wrote them letters encouraging them and continually pointing them toward Heavenly things. In this Scripture, Paul is virtually saying "God is meeting all my needs and He will meet yours, too!" The Heavenly point is that the people of Phillipi weren't rich, more likely in poverty, but Paul assures them that He (God) will exchange His glorious riches for theirs. We should follow Paul's example in pointing others to the eternal things and to "consider all things joy" (v. 4) and to the promise that He will take care of all our needs.

### Revisiting the Scripture
EXAMPLE: EVEN WHEN I lost my job, I knew that God would supply, fill me up so there was no more want, give me His riches in place of mine.

Your Story (write out the scripture following your EVEN WHEN moment as in the example):

## Remembering

After your EVEN WHEN moment, I'm sure you received a lot of well-meaning questions. Not well thought out, but definitely meant as a caring thought of how you were doing. With this Scripture in mind, I knew that God would supply all my needs, and I could simply ask for His covering while He worked that out. Most of the time, it was an abundance of riches that He lavished on me, but sometimes it was just the RIGHT amount. Can you think of a time after your EVEN WHEN moment when God supplied your needs? Write it in the space allotted so you will remember, and you can share it with family, friends, and future generations.

## Praying the Scripture

Father, I am so grateful that You call me your own and that You take care of me. Specifically, individually, completely. What a gracious father that You promised to take care of ALL my needs. All of the big ones, all of the tiniest of needs, all from Your riches that go beyond what I could even imagine. Thank you.

Yes and Amen

## GOD WILL FIGHT FOR YOU
He promises you.

*"The Lord will fight for you, and you have only to be silent."* Exodus 14:14 (ESV)

### Researching the Scripture

*"The Lord will fight for you"*- the Lord God Almighty will (future tense) do battle for me? Against who? In Exodus, where this scripture is found, Moses is trying to console the Israelites by reminding them that God brought them out of Egypt and even though the Egyptian armies were chasing them, God would provide a way out. They were grumbling and scared, surrounded on all sides by obstacles, and they needed to be reminded of how faithful God was to them. Moses, knowing it was God who brought them to this place, also knew God would fight for them and bring them out of Egypt. He wanted the people to know that as surely as he did. So, you might say "that's in the Old Testament and doesn't apply to here and now." Really? The things the Lord provided for the Israelities (columns of fire by night and a pillar of cloud by day to guide them, manna on a daily basis, the parting of the Red Sea so they could escape the Egyptians) were only for the Old Testament people? I don't think so. Every

day, we see God's fingerprints on the things He's working on if we will just look. And the fight? In this scripture, it was about flesh and blood enemies, but we know there is a Heavenly battle going on for us as well as on earth. We battle daily with preconceived notions, evil deeds, deception in the political realms, blindness when it comes to moral issues. God is in the midst of those things, too, and wants us to call upon His name to step in.

"*And you have only to be silent*"- Usually, there is an action that God wants us to take; there are also a few instances when He says "just be quiet." The Matthew Henry Commentary puts this in beautiful form- "He directs them to leave it to God, in a silent expectation of the event: *"Stand still,* and think not to save yourselves either by fighting or flying; wait God's orders, and observe them; be not contriving what course to take, but follow your leader; wait for God's appearances, and take notice of them, that you may see how foolish you are to distrust them. Compose yourselves, by an entire confidence in God, into a peaceful prospect of the great salvation God is now about to work for you. Hold your peace; you need not so much as give a shout against the enemy, as Jos. 6:16. The work shall be done without any concurrence of yours."[5] Just be still.

---

5

https://www.blueletterbible.org/Comm/mhc/Exd/Exd_014.cf m?a=64014

### Revisiting the Scripture

Example: EVEN WHEN it feels like my enemies are prospering, God was/is fighting for me and against any enemy that may come to steal, kill, or destroy me. EVEN WHEN, I only have to be silent and let God fight the battles.

Your Story (write out the scripture following your EVEN WHEN moment as in the example):

EVEN WHEN

### Remembering

Can you think of a time after your EVEN WHEN moment that God fought a battle for you, and you only had to stay silent? Maybe it was a situation that you had no control over, or maybe you did have the ability to interfere, but chose to let God handle it in His perfect timing and way. Write it down in the space allotted so you can remember and share it with others.

### Praying the Scripture

Father, you are such a good, good father. I forget that you go before me, and circle around behind me, and cover me on every side against the enemy, both seen and unseen. I forget so easily that I only have to be silent and let you fight my battles. Help me to remember that you've got this and by being quiet and letting You do your thing, I have confidence that You

are for me. Thank you for fighting for me.
Yes and Amen

## GOD PROVIDES FREEDOM
He promises you.

*"So if the Son sets you free, you are truly free."*
John 8:36 (NLT)

*"But if we confess our sins to Him, He is
faithful and just to forgive us our sins and to
cleanse us from all wickedness."* 1 John 1:9 (NLT)

### Researching the Scripture
*"So if the Son sets you free"*- Some translations use the word "makes" instead of "sets," which changes the scripture to read "so if the Son (capitalized to indicate Jesus) makes you free." *"Makes"* in the Greek indicates liberation or deliverance.

*"You are truly free"*- Free from sin. Delivered from a spirit of condemnation. Liberated in every shape and form that hinders you from doing God's work. BUT this freedom only comes "if the Son sets you free." He was never bound to slavery in sin like we are. Because we are no longer slaves or servants, but rather a part of the family, and because we believe that we are such, we are "truly free."

*"But if we confess our sins to Him"*- The word "confess" in the Greek is *homologeō* and means to

not deny or to admit or declare oneself guilty of what one is accused of. It can also mean to speak freely. To speak freely of our sins? That would mean we'd have to recognize them as sins first and foremost. And what sins are the scriptures referring to? Back to the Greek.

*"Sins"*-Hamartia= to miss the mark, to err, to violate God's law, to wander from or miss the path of uprightness or honor. Wait, to wander away from the path of uprightness and honor is sin? I think I do that every day. Ugh.

*"He is faithful and just to forgive us our sins"*- Faithful, aka worthy of trust. Just, aka righteous (or the Greek meaning- used of him whose way of thinking, feeling, and acting is wholly conformed to the will of God). Ugh, again. But then the Good News! Forgiven. He sends away...departs...lets go of our sin. Thank you, Jesus.

*"And to cleanse us from all wickedness"*- And just (different meaning!) like God, He takes it one step further, He cleanses.

### Revisiting the Scripture
EXAMPLE: EVEN WHEN my sins are exposed and it appears my friends have abandoned me, you have set ME free from the bondage of sin. If I will confess these sins to you (things I was thinking or doing or saying), you are faithful to forgive me and to cleanse me from all sin.

Your Story (write out the scripture following your EVEN WHEN moment as in the example):

### Remembering

I know there were times I doubted God after my EVEN WHEN moment. I know there were times when I thought things that weren't true, not honorable, and certainly off the path of righteousness. But when I confessed these things to God (he already knew- it was my act of humbling my pride, lowering my guard, and relying on Him instead), He was ready and waiting to walk away from it and not mention it, wipe my slate clean. Such a fresh wind comes with that cleansing! Do you remember a time after your EVEN WHEN moment where you just needed to 'fess up and lay it before God so you could feel "clean" and whole again? Write that time in the allotted space. It happens daily for me, which is why I always try to incorporate this system in my prayer life: Praise, Repent. Ask. Yield. You got it- P.R.A.Y.

### Praying the Scripture

Father, thank you that you provide a way to become righteous again through the confessing of our sins. During my EVEN WHEN moment, and to be honest on a daily basis before and after then, you have been faithful to wipe my slate clean and set me back on that path again. Forgive me for being selfish and unaware and bull-headed when it comes to sin. I yield to what you have in store for me from this moment forward. In Jesus Name.

Yes and Amen

## GOD CALMS FEAR
He promises you.

"*Now may the Lord of peace himself give you peace at all times in every way.*" 2 Thessalonians 3:16a (ESV)

### Researching the Scripture
"*Now may the Lord of peace himself*"- Peace-a state of tranquility, security, harmony.

"*Give you peace*"- That same peace is granted…offered…extended…supplied to YOU.

"*At all times and in every way.*"- Can't be more descriptive than that, can we? Every way and at all times.

Anxiety and fear are tough to overcome simply because they usually start in your mind. I know there is anxiety and fear in the world for all kinds of reasons. God in His infinite wisdom knows that, too, and gave us this scripture. The passion translation scripture (Psalm 94:19) says this, "Whenever my busy thoughts were out of control, the soothing comfort of your presence calmed me down and overwhelmed me with delight."

### Revisiting the Scripture
EXAMPLE: EVEN WHEN life is overwhelming, my anxieties are ramped up, and fear is creeping in, I know that the God of peace offers His peace.

Your Story (write out the scripture following your EVEN WHEN moment as in the example):

### Remembering
Numerous times (too many to count) I have struggled with anxiety and fear, especially after the EVEN WHEN moment. Am I making the right decision? Will this decision affect the next decision? What was the decision again? Some days, it takes loud music to distract me, sometimes no music. Sometimes I can't sleep because of the noise in my head. Multiple times I would just put worship music on and let it play for 24 hours, allowing that soaking worship to join with my prayers. And then, only when I'd turned it all over to God, His peace would wash over me. Write down a time when something similar happened to you.

### Praying the Scripture
Father, there is so much in this world to be anxious and fearful about, things in our control and things outside our control. When we begin to wrestle with those things, and our shoulders get tight, and our gut starts behaving badly, remind us to come to you. Switch out our anxieties and fears for Your peace.

We gladly accept this promise.
Yes and Amen

JULIE BROWN

# GOD WILL GUIDE YOU
He promises you.

*"The Lord says, "I will instruct you and teach you in the way you should go; I will counsel you with my eye upon you."* Psalm 32:8 (ESV)

### Researching the Scripture

*"The Lord says"*- Straight from His mouth to your ear…and mind…and soul.

*"I will instruct you"*- The Hebrew word for instruct is *śākal* and means a variety of things that I did not know: to be circumspect or to wisely understand, to prosper, to have insight and comprehension. This is where those grammar lessons come in handy. The "I" at the beginning of the sentence is the subject of the verb "instruct". So, this part of the scripture, if you turn that verb into adjectives could read "I [who has the insight and wise understanding and comprehension of the situation] will tell you." Knowing that God will impart the insight and wise understanding and comprehension to me is a game changer. I want (and need) a counselor who fully understands and comprehends and wants me to prosper in knowledge to counsel me.

73

"*And teach you*"- "Teach" is a different Hebrew word (*yārâ)* so you guessed it, means something different from "instruct", two words I put in the same category before this research. "Teach" means "to cast" or "point out". They could be synonyms, each with their own twist.

"*In the way you should go*."- On this journey I'm constantly on, which is fraught with choices, I'm thankful the way is defined by "should's". Not "will go" like a slave or servant, but like a parent who lovingly directs.

"*I will counsel you*"- This is a deliberate counsel together, not just a "do what I say". "There may be options and I'm going to advise you on the best plan or move for you."- my interpretation only.

"*With my eye upon you*."- Figuratively speaking, this includes not only His eye (attention), but includes so much more. Dr. James Strong, author of *Strong's Definitions*, defines the "Eye" in this scripture as equated to a picturesque fountain that is the eye of the landscape. His eye incorporates more than just the center focal of the picture, but its surroundings, the mental and emotional feeling, the countenance of the "fountain", if you will.[6] That's a lot more than just a mother watching out for her babies. A lot.

Love it when my Counselor has the play book and gives me instructions from it. Me, and everyone else, but me specifically. My plans, my needs, my path. And yours too.

---

[6] https://www.blueletterbible.org/lexicon/h5869/nlt/wlc/0-1/

**Revisiting the Scripture**

EXAMPLE: EVEN WHEN I've lost my way and feel so far from God, You are laying out the way I should go, giving direction and pointing to the best path, because you are constantly, and consistently, "watching" out for me.

Your Story (write out the scripture following your EVEN WHEN moment as in the example):
EVEN WHEN

**Remembering**

There are often many choices after your EVEN WHEN moment, so many that it often becomes overwhelming. In this scripture, we find that He is always wanting to cast and devise our plans and is willing to share them with us if we will only ask and listen. Can you think of a time when you had a decision to make, and you asked God "What am I supposed to do?" How did He answer? With a whisper? With a nudge? With a great big sign that was handed to you by a complete stranger or a close friend? Write it down in the space allotted.

(Maybe you haven't heard an answer yet. Keep this scripture close at hand. He will. He promises to instruct and guide you.)

**Praying the Scripture**

Father, I am so humbled by the care and attention you provide for me. You already know my future and yet, you take the opportunity to whisper in my ear, "You should go this way". If I'd only ask. Thank you for providing choices even when you know what we're going to do. Thank you for those gentle nudging and those not-so-subtle 4 a.m. wake ups because you want us to listen. Thank you for always having your eye upon me.

Yes and Amen

## GOD ANSWERS
He promises you.

*"Call to me and I will answer you, and will tell you great and hidden things that you have not known."* Jeremiah 33:3 (ESV)

### Researching the Scripture

*"Call to me"*- If you're a parent reading this, you know that call: Mom! Dad! This is the same usage; God wants us to call out to him. "Call" in this scripture includes: "to invite" or "summon".

*"And I will answer you"*- No meaning here to reveal; it's a simple (yet weighty) sentence. You call, He answers.

*"And will tell you"*- "Tell" in the Hebrew is *nāḡaḏ,* a pretty big word with lots of meanings. *Nāḡaḏ* means to announce, proclaim, to publish or acknowledge.

*"Great and hidden things"*- Great in magnitude and intensity. Secret things that have been cut off from view.

*"That you have not known."*- You haven't had the knowledge of these things before now. You didn't even know they existed.

Let's put this scripture in context. This is the

word that Jeremiah received to comfort the people of Jerusalem and to remind them that they only had to pray and He [God] would answer them. Despite this being a word to Jeremiah, I believe it is recorded in scripture as a promise to us, too, in this day and age. He still answers prayer when we call out to Him. He still reveals things to us that were initially hidden or unknown if we simply ask.

### Revisiting the Scripture

EXAMPLE: EVEN WHEN I've made a bad decision and the consequences have caught up to me, all I have to do is call out to my Heavenly Father, and He will provide answers and direction on paths that I probably can't see (or chose not to see) or discovered before.

Your Story (write out the scripture following your EVEN WHEN moment as in the example):

### Remembering

Can you think of a time when you called out to Him, and He dropped the answer right into your mind? Or when you called out to Him, and a person came on your path and enlightened your focus? Or when you called out to Him, and something you'd never seen before (didn't even know it existed) jumped into your eyesight? Write it down so you'll remember that when you call, He answers.

**Praying the Scripture**

Father, We are so thankful that you know much more than we do and you'll grant us your vision if we just ask for it. Thank you for being faithful and always answering us.

Yes and Amen

JULIE BROWN

## GOD TEACHES US
He promises you.

*"Teach me to do your will, for you are my God! Let your good spirit lead me on level ground!"*
Psalm 143:10 (ESV)

### Researching the Scripture
*"Teach me to do your will"*- Skillfully instruct and train me.

*"For you are my God."*- Is He truly? Proclaim that… say it out loud.

*"Let your good spirit lead me"*- Pretty straight forward in the Hebrew. God is good and wants to guide us if we allow Him to.

*"On level ground."*- Ah, here's the gold nugget I love discovering. "Level" is the Hebrew word *mîšôr* and means "upstanding" and together with the word "ground", it means a *level place* (free from obstacles), figurative for place of safety, comfort, and prosperity.[7] In contrast to a crooked place or a "bent" person.

### Revisiting the Scripture

---

[7] https://www.blueletterbible.org/lexicon/h4334/nlt/wlc/0-1
Brown-Driver-Briggs Lexicon

EXAMPLE: EVEN WHEN I am unsure of my future, I am reminded that my God is good and will skillfully instruct and train me in the things He has for me. He will point me to the path of righteousness and set me on a space that is level.

Your Story (write out the scripture following your EVEN WHEN moment as in the example):

### Remembering
Do you remember a time when you cried out to God, "teach me what you want me to know?" And He did just that? He brought you to a level place so that you could walk uprightly? Write it down in the allotted place so you can remember and share what God has done.

### Praying the Scripture
Father, thank you for teaching me your will on all things and for caring enough about me to provide skillful, targeted training so that I will know what you want me to do. Lead and guide me to those places free of obstacles where I feel safe, can prosper, and am comforted. I know challenges will come, but you promise those level places, too.

Yes and Amen

## YOU HAVE AN ENEMY AND
## EVERLASTING LIFE
He promises you.

*"The thief comes only to steal and kill and destroy. I came that they may have life and have it abundantly."* John 10:10 (ESV)

### Researching the Scripture

*"The thief"*- Thief. Embezzler. False Prophet. Pilferer. Enemy.

*"Comes"*- Note the "s" on the end of "comes"-present tense verb- the here and now.

*"Only"*- The Greek word is *"mē"* and "expresses an absolute denial".[8] The enemy cannot do anything but the following...

*"to steal and kill and destroy."*- to take away, to slaughter, to slay, to abolish, to ruin. Get the picture? If not, here's the final thought- to render useless. That's what this is about: rendering YOU useless.

*"I came"*- Same form of the word "come", but in past tense. He's already come and laid down His

---

8

https://www.blueletterbible.org/lexicon/g3361/esv/mgnt/0-1/ Strong's Definitions Legend

life for yours.

"*That they may have life*"- Sometimes words in scripture mean exactly what they are (ie. "that" is a normal conjunction) and sometimes, if you dig deep in the Greek, you find additional meaning to the word or its root word. "May have" is one of these nuggets. A seemingly innocent verb. Let me share with you what it is translated from the Greek- "to have (hold) in the hand, in the sense of wearing, to have (hold) possession of the mind (refers to alarm, agitating emotions, etc.), to hold fast keep, to have or comprise or involve, to regard or consider or hold as or own or possess."[9] Does that add to your thoughts about this scripture? Wait, there's more. "Life" in this same scripture is defined as "real and genuine, a life active and vigorous, devoted to God, blessed, in the portion even in this world of those who put their trust in Christ,"

"*and have it abundantly*."- The verb "have" is the same one as above, to hold in possession. "Abundantly" brings up all thoughts of Thanksgiving to me as in the table (and counter and side buffet) are laden with an overflow of food. Abundantly. God wants you to have a life that extraordinary, exceedingly above, much more than ever before. And with that abundance, we know that life flows into everlasting life if we've accepted Jesus to be our Savior.

Don't normally see those two promises together,

---

9

https://www.blueletterbible.org/lexicon/g2192/esv/mgnt/0-1/ Outline of Biblical Usage

do you? Because of the second (everlasting life), the first (the enemy) is coming for you. BUT he can ONLY do those things (steal, kill, and destroy) although he's deceptive and conniving and will try to mirror God's goodness as a deceiving spirit. BUT, because of God's Son laying down His life for us, we cannot only have everlasting life, BUT we can also live life to the fullest while here on earth. That's some good news.

I'd be amiss if I didn't make this comment here: The enemy is alive and well, looking for ways to deceive you. Always, always, ALWAYS test what people tell you (and what you tell yourself) against scripture. If it isn't what God would think about you, it's not truth. Keep your eyes open for the things that don't line up with what God says, half-truths included. The devil can ONLY lie, but it's often disguised in half-truths to break off chunks in your foundation. I'll say it again, always test words, feelings, actions up against what God says.

### Revisiting the Scripture
EXAMPLE: EVEN WHEN my husband dies, and my (and your) enemy tries to steal, kill, and destroy my life in every which way, He has promised me abundant and everlasting life.

Your Story (write out the scripture following your EVEN WHEN moment as in the example):

### Remembering

"You're not smart enough." "Who do you think you are speaking into other people's lives and telling them it was from God?" "What makes you so special?" "You will never be able to [insert your own word]." All lies, which means they come from the devil. What lie did you believe that God showed you was untrue? Or what scheme for destruction was averted when God revealed His truth to you? Write it in the space allotted.

### Praying the Scripture

Father, we know there's a war waging not only for our eternal souls, but also for the here and now, on this earth. The enemy would like nothing more than to have us believe lies or destroy the plans you have for us. We are so thankful that You gave us your Word to hold up against his attacks, that you want us to have an abundant life overflowing from Your goodness, and that you provide a way (accepting you as our Savior and Lord) to spend eternity with you.

Yes and Amen

# (PROMISE-
## your word/phrase)
### He promises you.

Time for a little research on your own. At the beginning of this workbook, you were asked to write down a word or phrase that best describes you right now or after your EVEN WHEN moment. In all of the promises God gave us in His Word, there is one that matches your word/phrase. Do a little research and use the format from the other promises to write out your own.

Scripture:

**Researching the Scripture**: (tear down the scripture in bite-sized pieces and look the words up in a Greek or Hebrew translation like the Blue Letter Bible does.)

**Revisiting the Scripture**

Your Story (write out the scripture following your EVEN WHEN moment as in the examples from previous promises):

**Remembering**
(Remember a time that clearly pictures your promise and scripture? Write it down here.)

**Praying the Scripture**
Write a prayer as we did with the other promises in the space allotted. Plug in your EVEN WHEN moment and follow the scripture.

Yes and Amen

## CONCLUSION

What a ride! Walking through His promises for us is so encouraging. We often think we have to go it alone, fight our battles, dig out of our sin, try not to be fearful or anxious, make all of the ends meet, protect ourselves…the list goes on and on. Why do we think that our Heavenly Creator wouldn't be interested in us after our creation? Why do we immediately think we have to do everything through our own power? Especially when we believe in God who is all-powerful, all-knowing, all-present, ALL EVERYTHING? So very thankful that I have surrendered my life to Jesus and He is in control. Not that I don't snatch that control back many, many times…daily, but that He loves us enough to give His only Son to die on the cross and provide a way to draw us to Him. It's not easy. He didn't promise that. But it's the only path I want to be on.

So now it's your turn. Everything that you've written in this workbook should be shared. Be transparent with others about your path and the journey He has you on. Tell the next generation how faithful God is and show them the promises and how He can meet them right where they're at, too.

My last words to you…

God is good. God is faithful.

THANK YOU

I am forever grateful that God gave me the book "God's promises are still true: EVEN WHEN" and followed up with this workbook. I am reminded every day of how blessed I am.

Thank you, Hannah, for reading this workbook of promises, correcting my grammar, and fact-checking my scriptures. You are truly a Bible scholar, not only because you have Biblical education under your belt, but because you love the Word. Be watchful and alert as the enemy wants to spin you out at every opportunity but be thankful and feel your worth and value as the strong Christ-follower that I know you are. Also, front cover photo creds to you!

Thank you, Mom, Daddy, and Jenn, for always being anxious to read what I've written. I am encouraged to be a better person and Jesus-lover with your support.

Thank you, Richard, for believing in me and supporting whatever I do. Your influence in my life is invaluable.

Thank you, Andrew, for your exhaustive work in dissecting my interpretations and causing this piece of work to be full of truth. Your encouragement and knowledge with grace (for my mistakes) was beyond my expectation.

Thank you, Cynthia, for taking a chance on me and encouraging me to write the "EVEN WHEN" book and this workbook "because people need this." (your words to me at that very first editor appointment)

Other books by Julie Brown:

Even When
Chained to a Dream Truth=Freedom, Book 1
COMING SOON: Chasing Truth
Truth=Freedom, Book 2

"To share your EVEN WHEN journey, please visit my website at www.juliebrown-author.com."

"I love comments and feedback from readers! Want to chat? Visit me at www.juliebrown-author.com or julie@juliebrown-author.com. I'd love to hear from you!"

BIO- Julie Brown became a widow in 2021 and has firsthand knowledge of how grief and loss can be an all-consuming, hard journey. She has also written a romantic suspense fiction series titled Truth=Freedom. Julie Brown writes from her back porch in Missouri where the hummingbirds fly, the coffee is sweet, and friends are welcomed.

www.ingramcontent.com/pod-product-compliance
Lightning Source LLC
Chambersburg PA
CBHW071209120626
46546CB00006B/2490